MW00710497

HOW TO HELP YOUR CHILD SUCCEED IN SCHOOL

BY

REYNOLD BEAN, ED.M.

Library of Congress Cataloging-in-Publication Date

Bean, Reynold, 1935-
How to help your child succeed in school / by Reynold Bean.

p. cm. — (The whole child series)

ISBN 0-8431-2871-2 :

1. Home and school—United States. 2. Education—United States-
-Parent participation. 3. Parent-teacher relationships—United States.
I. Title. II. Series.
LC225.3.B43 1991
371.1'03—dc20   90-25457
CIP

Published by Price Stern Sloan, Inc.
11150 Olympic Boulevard, Suite 650, Los Angeles, California 90064
10 9 8 7 6 5 4 3 2

Copyright 1991 by Price Stern Sloan, Inc.

PRICE STERN SLOAN
Los Angeles

CONTENTS

ACKNOWLEDGEMENTS

Special thanks to Carolyn McKennon, Dick Patterson, Mike James, Thom Dunks, Carl Pearson, Dave Schumaker, Liz Merriam, Penny Chesluk and Stan Bovee. To them and the teachers and employees of the Soquel Union Elementary School District, a special group who help children succeed in school, with love and respect.

INTRODUCTION

If all things are considered equal in life, how then is it that some people seem to lead more successful, productive and happier lives than others? What gives them the advantage? Much research has been done to determine which factors enhance a person's chance for success in life—be it in career, family or personal happiness. And, as is often the case with comparative studies, it's difficult to determine which factor is the more important. Some researchers believe strongly that one's ability to succeed is hereditary, the result of genetic traits passed down from successful parents to their children. Other's firmly believe the environment children are raised in is the determining factor. Still others believe it's a combination of both. Some children seem to be born with innate talent, above average intelligence, strong character and a favorable disposition. Others do not. But regardless of the socio-economic factors and the genetic makeup of the parents, every child in our day and age is presented with the same equal opportunity—a formal education. Rich or poor, inherited intelligence or otherwise, blue collar or white—every child is given the same opportunity to acquire the knowledge to help them lead productive lives as an adult. It is the child who makes the most of this opportunity that will be given the advantage, one that can mean the difference between success, mediocrity or failure.

This is not to say that failure in school means failure in life or vice versa. Certainly there are exceptions, people who didn't progress beyond grade school or performed poorly throughout their school years who were ultimately successful throughout their lives. Likewise, there are former class valedictorian's who haven't been so successful. Although it can't be definitely stated that success in school is directly related to success in life, it certainly can't hurt.

This book is about things that you can do to help your child succeed in school. As a teacher, administrator, consultant and school board member, I'm all too aware of the limitations of most schools, as well as their benefits, and that's why you must get involved in your children's education. You have to be an advocate for your children and give them guidance and support, yet you must also learn when to step back so that they will learn to assume responsibility for their own school success. Your children can't succeed without you, but you can't succeed for them, either.

You don't have to be a scholar nor even well educated to help your children succeed in school. You don't have to be rich. You don't have to be well read and possess a high IQ. You don't have to buy special learning devices. What you must have are reasonable expectations and a positive attitude. Your goal should be to develop within your children a strong desire to learn, a high level of self-esteem, a sense of responsibility and the self-confidence to perform the tasks required of school.

This book will help you manage your children's educational careers in ways that are most helpful to them and to the school and teachers. You will learn how to use the school's resources for your children's benefit. You will learn a few techniques for getting around school bureaucracies and rules so they won't deny your children of important opportunities.

How To Help Your Children Succeed In School, is chiefly addressed to the needs of children in elementary and middle school grades, because that's when you should begin preparing your children to succeed. A child* who needs help in secondary school may be one whose parents didn't give him proper guidance when he was just starting out. Give your child a good start.

Reynold Bean
Aptos, California

ACKNOWLEDGMENT

It was a splendid evening. A beautiful home, inspiring company and wonderful food prepared by Santa Cruz's champion caterer. Time to talk about kids and schools. Who better to help me than people who have been helping kids succeed in school for years. Carolyn McKennon, Dick Patterson, Mike James, Thom Dunks, Carl Pearson, Dave Schumaker, Liz Merriam, Penny Chesluk, and Stan Bovee—Superintendents, Administrators, and Master Teachers. By any measures, outstanding educators, who have demonstrated their love for children and joyful commitment to the task of educating them. They have shown that Educator is a noble and honorable calling, when it is done right. To them and the teachers and employees of the Soquel Union Elementary School District, in Santa Cruz County, California, a special group who help children succeed in school, year after year, with love and respect.

---

*"He," rather than "he or she" is used throughout the text for the sake of fluidity.

Section I

The Basic Skills Children Need to be Successful in School

1

Responsibility: the Key to Success

Responsibility is not genetic. It has to be learned through experience (for more detail on responsibility, see *How To Teach Children Responsibility* of *The Whole Child Series*). Children must do what's required to be successful in school, but most of it doesn't require superior intelligence. Although being bright gives children an advantage in school, being able to take responsibility gives them a greater advantage. Very bright kids who lack a sense of responsibility or commitment to their own learning set themselves up for failure and are no fun to teach, whether they're in kindergarten or high school.

It's hard to hold back children who have a good sense of responsibility. They will do well at most things that they try. Children who have a sense of responsibility instilled in them when they're young will succeed in what they do, even during rebellious periods when they get older. Kids who are irresponsible drive teachers batty. All children are irresponsible some of the time. It's part of growing up.

DEFINING RESPONSIBILITY

Most adults consider a child responsible if he is doing what they *think* he should be doing. This view isn't entirely wrong, although it becomes limiting and harder to apply to older children.

The essence of being responsible is to be able to make independent choices and decisions to do what's appropriate in any situation. The *independent decisions* part of this definition is evidence that responsible children don't need adults telling them what to do all the time, but know what's expected of them and do it. The *appropriate* part of the definition gets confusing because it depends on the individual's definition of what is appropriate. Everyone has a different viewpoint.

Children in the early years of school must depend on adults to give them proper guidance about what is appropriate in most situations. As they get older, we expect them to have a better sense of what's appropriate and act accordingly. But as children get older, they should be developing their own values about right and wrong and begin to explore alternatives, some of which adults may consider *inappropriate*. That's when things begin to get confusing. Responsible behavior then becomes more subjective, open to discussion, rather than behavior based on hard and fast rules.

3

RESPONSIBILITY IN THE CLASSROOM

Children who are taught to be responsible at home have learned how to plan, organize and assume the consequences for their actions, good or bad. Most chores at home need to be done at certain times, under certain conditions, and there should be consequences for not doing them. Children find a similar situation at school. Learning tasks occur at certain times, must be done in certain ways, and there are consequences for not doing things correctly. Children who have had to deal with this before will not find school a foreign experience. They will be more familiar with the process, and therefore more comfortable. Many, if not most, children who develop learning problems early in their schooling, were never comfortable with it in the beginning.

Children who have learned to do the right thing on their own without being told by an adult will stand a much better chance at succeeding in school than the children who must be constantly told what to do. This is so for a simple reason: Most classrooms operate on a 30:1 student/teacher ratio. That's 30 students and one teacher. Sometimes there are aides to help, but the teacher obviously can not hold the hand of every child at the same time. Children who have learned how to conduct themselves without constant adult directives will take the initiative to work problems out on their own. They will move quickly on to the next task, and look for extra work to keep them busy if they should finish early, rather than wait for the teacher to lead them by the hand through each activity! This trait generates favorable attention from the teachers, who absolutely love children who perform their work without depending on them all the time.

RESPONSIBILITY HELPS CHILDREN COPE WITH STRESS

For many children, school can be a very stressful place. Children are continually faced with many decisions, such as:

- Where does this go?
- Do I put this here or there?
- Which is the correct answer, this or that?
- Am I finished or not?
- What color should I use?
- What should I do next?
- How should I handle this kid who is bothering me?
- Should I ask the teacher for help?

Fear of failing, fear of other children, fear of appearing foolish, embarrassment about personal characteristics, fear of disapproval, fear of approval and many other factors can also induce stress in children, whether they are founded on real experiences or imagination. Children who can't cope with stress often have a hard time retaining learned material and develop learning or behavior problems.

4

On the other hand, children who have learned to take responsibility for important matters (relative to their age and development) have had some experience in coping with stress, which makes them more prepared to handle it in school. The child who has already learned to make decisions and assume responsibility for duties, rules and chores at home will have a considerable advantage in handling learning situations without excessive stress at school. They'll start using these skills from the first day in kindergarten, when the teacher says, "Come now children, let's all sit in the circle, hold hands, quiet down and listen to this story." I know quite a few adults that couldn't do all that without making a fuss!

TEACHING CHILDREN RESPONSIBILITY

If children have been properly taught to handle responsibilities at home, they have been taught how to do things right. Doing things right means that a clear standard has been established and the child has been taught effective ways to meet it. He has been allowed to make mistakes, learn from them, evaluate and correct his own performance.

Teaching children to be responsible not only builds character, but results in a set of complex and sophisticated skills that are crucial to success in school. Teaching children to be responsible begins when you first expose them to the idea that picking up after themselves makes Mom and Dad incredibly happy! This first experience should occur long before your children are ready for school. If you consistently apply good methods for teaching responsibility, children will have considerable experience performing tasks similar to what they will have to do in school.

If you hadn't done these things before your child started school, and you are beginning to see the results in poor performance and attitudes about school, don't wait any longer. It's never too late to help a child learn to be responsible, although the longer you wait, the harder it becomes to teach them. As I mentioned at the beginning of this chapter, see *How To Teach Children Responsibility* from *The Whole Child Series* for more detailed information.

2

Creating the Desire to Learn

Helping children to be successful in school is an easy task if they really *want* to learn. In fact, if a child has a strong desire to learn, and firmly believes that school is important work, then success is virtually guaranteed. But this attitude rarely comes naturally. Attitudes are developed, not inherited, and it is your responsibility to develop a positive attitude about school in your children.

However, it's hard to get a child to love learning for its own sake. Some children love to learn, some love to do and others love to be. If a child doesn't like to learn, but is motivated strongly to succeed, then he still has an excellent chance of being successful. Schooling and learning are not necessarily the same thing. Schooling is the process of meeting the requirements imposed by that institution in a way that allows a child to be successful in moving through it. So your goal is to instill a positive attitude in your children and give them the motivation to do well in school—as early as possible.

GETTING READY FOR KINDERGARTEN

There are many things that you can do to prepare your children for kindergarten. While working on some of their basic skills is helpful, it should not be the most important goal on your mind. You should concentrate on developing your children's attitude to the point that they can't wait to go when the day comes! What follows are some helpful suggestions on things you should and shouldn't do to get them ready.

Things You Should Do

- Talk about school in positive ways. Point it out as you pass one, when you're watching TV where kids are going to school and on other occasions. Always try to relay very happy, positive experiences you had in school to your child—favorite football games, favorite teachers, good friends, sports you participated in, clubs and so forth.

- As the time for kindergarten nears begin household routines that will support going to school. These can include more stringent rules for bedtime, quiet times for reading and playing that can become homework time later. Place more emphasis on books and other tools of schooling—pencils, drawing, maps—and point out to your children that they will see more of these things when they go to school.

- Start going to the library if you have not done so before. Libraries provide an excellent environment to develop good attitudes about books and reading. Many communities sponsor a "Children's Story Hour" type of program, usually at no charge, where you can drop your children off for a fun storytelling session with other children their age. If you don't have a library nearby, increase the number of books and magazines in your house, to the extent that your budget permits. You don't have to buy a set of encyclopedias!

- Although it may not seem like it to you, a school appears gigantic to a kindergartner, with hallways a mile long, rooms as big as a football field and thousands of kids—a pretty intimidating, scary place. So take your child to a school to show him what it's like well before he begins, to de-mystify it and allow him to adjust to the size, noise and confusion.

- Once you know your child's room assignment, take him to meet the teacher before the first day, so that on the first day he won't be meeting a total stranger. Insist that you and your child meet his first teacher, even if the school feels that it's an imposition!

- Play "going to school" with your children from time to time. Spend a little time teaching them letters or numbers, emphasizing that so much more about them will be learned in school. Help them identify words in books that you read to them. You don't have to teach them to read, but you're helping them to discover that they can learn. That's more important for them to know; they'll learn to read quickly at school if they have a good attitude about learning and are developmentally ready.

- Prepare a place for children's school things before they start school and maintain it after they begin. Have a place for their books, school supplies, clothes, lunch pail. Having a place for their school "stuff" is akin to Mom and Dad having a place for their work stuff. You should reinforce this comparison, because your children know work is important, and therefore will learn that their school is important too.

- Display your children's drawings or writings before they ever start school, and continue to do so with the projects that they bring home. A refrigerator is a good spot.

- Point out that many things that you enjoy are things that you first learned to do in school. Tell children stories about your school experiences. If you liked school, tell them why. If you didn't, tell them why you've come to think it's important.

- If you send your children to pre-school or a day care program, use the teachers as a resource for developing good attitudes about school. Let them know that you are concerned that your child have a good attitude about school before he goes.

- If you are working parents and have child care try to insure that those caretakers have a good attitude about school.

Things You Shouldn't Do

- Don't push your children academically prior to school. You shouldn't try to teach them to read or demand they count to one hundred, write out the alphabet, spell their name or identify geometric shapes and colors perfectly if your children are reluctant, uncomfortable or struggle with learning these things. If your children are enthusiastic about it, fine. But if children are reluctant to learn, and you push them to succeed and they fail, they will learn to associate this failure with school. No one likes to fail! Allow your children to develop naturally. Give them encouragement and guidance, create an environment that gives them the opportunity to develop their skills at their own pace. Don't overdo it, and don't express any disappointment if they fail to live up to your expectations. Your children will sense this disappointment, causing them to fear failure to the point where they are afraid to try. Much of learning has to do with failure—in order to learn what is right, a child must also learn what is wrong.

- Don't assume that your child is ready for kindergarten just because he reaches a certain age. If your child is to develop a positive attitude about school, he must be socially and emotionally developed enough to handle it. A high level of intelligence does not guarantee readiness. To be sure, have your child given a "kindergarten readiness test" which is usually offered by the school.

- Don't invest in things such as talking computers, early learning book programs or other teaching aids thinking they will ensure your child will do well in school. While such aids have some merit, your positive attitude and support of your child has been shown through research to have the most effect. It's inexpensive too!

- Don't try to teach your children what you believe they will need to know in school. You may assume that your schooling was like your child's will be. You are most likely wrong! The world today is far different than it was when you entered school, and no less so than in education. Yes, children are still taught the "three R's," but in many schools they are also exposed to the basics of computer technology, even in primary grades! Don't give them expectations that may prove to be false—it will only add to their confusion.

- Don't use other children as examples of the virtue of schooling. Your children may develop the idea that they have to be like those children in order to be successful. Don't use bright older siblings as standards or examples. The pressure to measure up to those higher standards right away could lead to failure and ultimately, a low self-esteem.

OVERCOMING CRITICISM OF SCHOOL

Children are often exposed to many negative comments about school, which makes it harder for them to view it as a positive experience. They may have experiences that lead them to believe school is a waste of time. There are even some school people who don't think that well of it, though it's the way they earn their living. Children may get teachers who are misplaced and make learning a tortuous task. They may have siblings or relatives who have bad attitudes about school, or you yourself may have had bad experiences in school that you convey to your child, consciously or not. Your attitude about school and the manner in which it is communicated has a powerful effect on how your children feel about it when they start. Their own experiences will influence their attitudes as they move through the grades. This means that you may have to work harder as time goes on to keep the belief of school's importance before them. You'll probably argue about it from time to time, but that will communicate how important you feel it to be.

Developing positive attitudes about school is one of the most important things you can do as a concerned, involved parent. When combined with a good sense of responsibility, you'll have prepared your child with an excellent chance to succeed in school.

3

How Important is Intelligence?

The nature of intelligence has been the subject of heated debate among scientists, researchers and scholars for centuries. Although much is understood about intelligence at this time, new theories and studies continue to challenge old ones. There is still a question as to how much of an individual's intellect is inherited and how much is developed. It is still uncertain whether the intellect children possess genetically is all they're going to have. They may be able to pick some more up along the way, if you do the right things.

TYPES OF INTELLIGENCE

Some observers believe there are different kinds of intelligence. Casual observation would seem to confirm that notion. Some people who weren't very bright in school have gone on to lead successful, productive lives; and we all know of "school brains" who aced every test but couldn't deal with many of the practical aspects of life necessary for success. Having children who don't have star quality intelligence is no sign that they are doomed to a loser's life.

Verbal intelligence is a very useful sort to have in school, because so much of school learning depends on language. Much of what is known as "high intellect" is verbal intelligence, information that is learned or expressed verbally. There is most likely a *creative intelligence*, which allows people to see new possibilities in ordinary sources of information. There is definitely an *analytical intelligence* which permits people to see logical pieces of whole processes and manipulate them in various ways. *Expressive intelligence* has to do with being able to find appropriate forms for demonstrating one's own unique combination of thoughts and feelings in ways that communicate them to others. Good athletes seem to have a *physical intelligence* which allows them to have good coordination between the mind's intention and the body's ability to carry it out. *Artistic intelligence* is about being able to find ways to translate imagination into some satisfying material form. *Problem-solving intelligence* is reflected in a person's practical approach to devising solutions to problems that arise in ordinary living. *Perceptual intelligence* is demonstrated by people who learn to see things that others miss. There are many kinds of intelligence and all children have lots of some and less of others.

As schools become more familiar with the various kinds of intelligence that children possess and design programs to develop the different types, children who might not otherwise be highly successful in school will find more ways to succeed.

I.Q. TESTS

The relative merit of I.Q. tests is another subject quite often debated among psychologists and educators. But the general consensus is that a child's I.Q. is not the only factor that will determine the quality of his life.

I suffered for a long time from this I.Q. business. I was not a star student during most of my schooling, in fact I was what is known as a "behavior problem." On one of my escapades, I engineered a "break-in" to the school's records room. Several of my impressionable buddies and I checked out our files, which were secret documents in those days. Our I.Q. scores were prominently displayed on the jacket of the folders. Despite being the leader of the gang, my score was the lowest of my group. It was a rather ordinary score. I suffered, secretly, for many years thinking that I did not have the requisite intelligence to be among the dominating intellects of my various schools. I counsel students not to break into school record offices unless they're ready for bad news!

I have had many days where that I.Q. score would have been considered inflated, relative to my performance, but on other days, I have been quite brilliant! I never had the courage, though, to have my I.Q. remeasured, nor have I ever seen the I.Q. scores of any of my children. The final word here is: don't place great value on I.Q. tests. They are not necessarily a true indicator of overall intelligence, and have little bearing as to whether or not your child will be successful in school.

As an argument in favor of positive attitude over intelligence, I'd like to relay another personal experience, keeping in mind what I just said about my I.Q. One year, when I was in high school, I was placed in an English class with the brightest students in the school. They were all National Honor Society students with very high grade point averages (GPA's). I was not. In fact, it remains a mystery to me today why I was ever placed in the class to begin with. I firmly resolved to hold my own, show these brainy guys and gals up if I could, not so much from a sense of nobility as from the dread of appearing a complete fool. This class ended up being the toughest of my curriculum, and I had to work extremely hard. The B that I received at the end of the semester meant more to me than the A's that the other kids achieved. Nobody expected me to do well, but my positive attitude and strong desire to succeed overcame any shortcomings I may have had in intelligence.

4

Success in School Depends on More than You Know

It's been said that the only difference between man and animal is man's ability to reason. Schooling isn't entirely about learning facts and figures, although it's hard to go far without them. Schooling is about *making sense* of facts and figures. Being successful in school depends on how well children *think* or *reason*, and not necessarily what they can recite from memory. If a child can think competently, the process of learning facts and figures happens automatically, provided it is adequately taught. Children who know how to think have a special advantage in school and it's a skill that parents can help children develop.

Understanding thinking sounds like a complex matter, the proper subject for a tome on the brain, not a handbook for helping your child be successful in school. Not so! It has to do with the ability to sort things out, find patterns in complex material, reason from a premise and make sense of things that aren't easy to make sense of. That, more or less, is what educators mean by the term "thinking skills." Many schools are devoting time and attention to developing these thinking skills, because they've discovered that kids don't do it well. Having a functioning brain is no guarantee that one will think straight, as anyone knows who has made a dumb mistake, overlooked something they should know or missed the point when they should have understood. It's not surprising that kids don't think straight consistently; it's something they need to learn.

COMMUNICATION

You don't have to be an educator or psychologist to help your children learn how to think in ways that will help them be successful in school. One of the more important steps to developing good thinking skills is *communication*. How you communicate with your children, and how language is used in your home, will help teach your children how to think.

Communication and language are fancy words to describe *talking* and *listening*, common enough terms most of us can relate to, some more than others. Children who are talked to and listened to with respect for their intelligence when they are young tend to think better when they are older. I don't mean you have to talk to your children like a scholar or academician, but you should talk to them frequently, take the time to thoroughly explain things they don't understand and listen to what they have to say. Most importantly, don't underestimate their ability to understand what you are saying! The point is to encourage and require children to talk about what they are thinking, thus helping them learn to be more competent thinkers.

The process should begin immediately following the birth of your child. Some psychologists believe it is beneficial to speak to your children while they are still in the womb. It is best to avoid the "gitchee gitchee goo" type of babble. You want your child to learn to speak as adults speak, and babbling incoherently to them translates as such. When an infant smiles when you babble, it is a reaction to *how*, rather than *what*, was said.

Don't Underestimate Your Child's Ability To Understand You

There is one common misconception you should avoid. Many adults do not believe infants and toddlers understand fully what is said to them, basing this opinion on how well toddlers can express themselves verbally. The fact is, a child's ability to comprehend develops faster than his ability to express what he is thinking verbally. That children talk so insistently, even before we can understand a word they say, is evidence that they're thinking even before they get the lingo straightened out—yet for the most part we still understand what they are saying. Many adults don't think children will understand if they speak to them like an adult, or explain a complex principle, albeit simply, in "real" language. But this isn't necessarily true. If children hear people using language properly they become much better at communicating complex thoughts and information. The more complex and sophisticated their language capability is, the more competent they will be at thinking.

PROBLEM SOLVING

When children have learned to communicate their needs and tell you what they want you to know, teaching them to think can begin in earnest. One of the most important things you can encourage children to do is to solve problems on their own. Thinking skills are preceded by learning effective problem-solving skills. Children learn these skills the old fashioned way: trial-and-error. From trial-and-error, they gain experience. Your job is to guide them by communicating; to analyze what they're doing, clarify what they want, help them to assess their resources and help them evaluate their results. Asking children to do chores and follow rules are beneficial to helping them think, because they have to become problem solvers in the process. You help children learn to think with the very same process used to help them become responsible. This is one reason why there is a close correlation between a child's sense of responsibility and his success in school.

Children learn a great deal about problem solving by watching their parents solve problems. If you approach a complex problem or situation with frustration or anger, then your child will likely develop a similar approach. Wise parents will take the time to explain to their children how they are going about solving a problem so that the children can learn how it's done. If you want your child to become an analytical, pragmatic thinker, then you must set the example by adopting the same method.

TELEVISION & THINKING

Although many will jump right in and say television and thinking is a contradiction in terms, it's not yet clear whether watching T.V. interferes with children learning to think well, although there are strong arguments both pro and con. What seems true is that excessive T.V. uses up time available for doing things that do improve thinking skills, the interactive things that are pointed out above. If too much T.V. watching stops parents and children from communicating with each other, thinking and success in school will be undermined.

OTHER BASIC SKILLS

Being successful in school requires skills that can be learned and reinforced at home. Here's a list of them:

- *Listening* is a skill that you can teach your children by insisting that they pay attention to what you have to say, and by paying attention to what they have to say.

- *Persistence* is a skill your children will learn when you require that they finish what they start and stick with things even though it is difficult.

- *Attention-to-Detail* is learned when you clarify standards, teach children how to do things well and monitor their performance fairly but consistently.

- *Sociability* is the skill of getting along with others. Children learn this skill from engaging in rich and satisfying relationships with people of many ages and circumstances. Present them with this opportunity as frequently as possible.

- *Trust* is a skill that children learn from being around people who are trustworthy—people who make promises and keep them, people who don't feed them information that turns out to be false or tell them lies. If children don't learn to know when to trust an adult and when not to, they will have a hard time trusting their teachers and accepting what they say.

19

- *Flexibility* is an attribute that children have when they have broad and diverse experiences in their lives. Parents don't have to be rich or educated to support, encourage and provide their children with a wide range of appropriate childhood experiences.

- *Self-discipline* is the skill of being able to think before you act, to control emotions and actions in order to successfully complete a task. Children learn self-discipline by living with adults who have self-discipline in a home environment that places importance on good behavior and sharing household functions.

These skills are not only basic to the process of preparing your child for school, they are also necessary for healthy child development. But the most important thing to consider is that your child won't learn these skills unless you set the example. You must listen, be persistent, pay attention-to-detail, be sociable, trustworthy, flexible and self-disciplined before you can demand that your child be all of these things.

THINGS YOU CAN DO AT HOME

There are many things you can do at home, starting long before a child is ready to go to school. Talk at meals, ask them questions, encourage your children to "say more." When they do, allow your children to have center stage when they explain things, give them plenty of time to say what's on their minds and express your opinions freely. You should even allow your children to argue, however you should encourage them to do so logically and rationally. Allow children to listen to adults, don't chase them away when family and friends are visiting. Allow them to participate in appropriate ways in adult conversations. Ask them to tell visiting relatives about their successes and interests. These are all methods you can use to teach your children to think.

Reading

Children whose parents read and enjoy reading (even in foreign languages) will be more likely to read and enjoy it themselves. The relationship to school success is obvious. Have reading material around the house, books, magazines, and newspapers. Set time for children to read and insist that they give you the opportunity to do so. Creating positive family values about reading is quite helpful in encouraging thinking skills in children. Reading to children is not only beneficial, but enjoyable as well.

Section II

Your Relationship to the School and Teacher

5

The Parent/Teacher Relationship

Have you ever been alone with 30 kids in a room for 6 hours, bearing the pressure and responsibility for their emotional, social and intellectual development, day after day, year after year? You can't begin to imagine what this might be like unless you are a teacher. Being a teacher is a complex, difficult job, a fact few people outside the educational process appreciate. Furthermore, teachers are human just like the rest of us. They are like people whom you meet in most walks of life. Some are courageous, others timid. Some are insightful, others less sensitive. Some are assertive, others shy. Some are convivial, others are not. You have to know your child's teachers as the real people they are.

I am biased in favor of teachers. You should know that from the start. The overwhelming majority of them like children, know how to handle them, and must cope with the emotional consequences of what many families are experiencing. Most teachers remain caring people despite being part of a complex bureaucracy. They do their best to give individual attention to many children despite the numbers that they must deal with. They are generally strong advocates for children's needs and they must deal with many parents and professionals. Teachers are the most important people in children's lives after the parents.

GET TO KNOW YOUR CHILD'S TEACHER

It's in your child's best interest that you have a good relationship with his teacher. Why? Because if the teacher knows and likes a child's parents, the chances are that teacher will be inclined to give that child a little extra attention. Many teachers reading the last sentence are screaming, "Foul!" The myth that teachers treat all children even-handedly is part of the illusion that they are super-human. No one treats everyone the same.

If teachers know and like a child's parent, this is what will likely happen:

- When a problem arises the parent is more likely to be called because the teacher doesn't feel as intimidated as they might with a "faceless" parent.

- If the teacher knows something about the family, i.e. the background, the educational and professional level of the parents, she will be more sensitive to the child's background and ability to

23

learn, and be able to adjust accordingly.

- Making the effort to get to know the teacher tells her that you are greatly concerned about your child's education, and she is likely to put forth extra effort to meet those expectations.

- Some teachers may favor your children with a second chance, the benefit of the doubt and a little more slack than other kids get if they know you well.

- When your children realize that the teacher knows and likes you and vice versa, they feel more secure, which motivates them to learn.

- If you know the teacher well, she will make an extra effort to pass on positive reports about how well your child is doing, which will help raise your child's self-esteem.

- "Do Unto Others As You Would Have Others Do Unto You." In other words, if you show a teacher respect and appreciation, it is likely they will show the same to you.

How do you develop a good relationship with a teacher? First, you must dispense with the idea that teachers are too busy to deal with you. All good teachers want the students' parents to be partners in their education. It makes their job easier and more satisfying. Many parents have only a vague idea of what teachers do. When you are not in the classroom it's hard to imagine how complex it is to manage. Teachers wish parents to understand how they do their jobs, because that will produce more respect and appreciation for what they do. Teachers, like most people, show appreciation for those who seem to appreciate them. Many actually believe that most parents aren't interested in what they do!

Teachers who seem to resist parental involvement are afraid that the parents will be overly critical and adverse to their goals—a sign of insecurity. If you meet this type of teacher, you'd be wise to make the extra effort to overcome this obstacle.

Things You Can Do

- Meet the teacher face-to-face before school starts in the Fall (they're around), early in the school year (within weeks of school starting) or drop in from time to time. Informal contacts are as good as formal ones.

- Send notes to the teacher occasionally which comment favorably on something that your child has told you about school.

- Ask for the teacher's advice in: choosing books for your child to read; suggestions for helping with homework; behavior management issues; dealing with negative attitudes about school; and anything else you can do to help your child perform better in school.

- Let the teacher know when your child has shown progress at home, such as when he picked out a word that he learned to read at school.

- Let the teacher know that you will check with her to verify some things your child may relate to you about school. Some children will manipulate a lack of communication between parents and teachers to their advantage.

- If you are a working parent, have an agreement with the teacher about when and where you can call each other to talk about your child. Many teachers are willing to be called at home if they have a prior arrangement with the parents. You may be able to be called at work.

You want your child to stand out to the teacher so as to be treated as an individual, not a number. Although most teachers will do the very best they can to give individual attention to every child, they are limited by the number of children they have to deal with. You have to be a special advocate for your own children, but by engaging the teacher in your purposes, by getting to know her and having her know and like you, your influence over your child's welfare is extended to school. It gives your child another advantage in becoming successful in school.

6

Getting Involved

Educators *want* parents to be involved with their children's schooling. They *want* parents to attend meetings, lectures, events and conferences conducted by the school. It's important that you attend as many of these events as possible, because it's to your child's advantage for you to do so.

By attending school events, you show that school is important to you. If you don't care, neither will your children. If you're more involved, attend all meetings, join the PTA and initiate conferences with the principal and teachers, you'll motivate your children more. Kids who aren't doing well in school would rather keep the school and their parents distant from each other. They recognize that if the teacher and parents support each other, they are going to be held more accountable for their performance. Likewise, educators are more likely to pay more attention to children whose parents are involved. Teachers do a better job when they think that they're being watched, especially those who have some room for improvement!

Another important reason to be involved with school is to evaluate for yourself what children say about school, their teachers and the other kids. Or you can find out if what the *teachers* are telling you is true. It's difficult to know how to respond to your child's complaints about school. When you know the people involved you can be more objective about what your children say. You need to know whether what they say is generally true or only reflects their individual experience. As children advance through the grades they report less about what goes on, reserving it as their "private life." Staying in touch with the school allows you to have other sources of information besides your children's reports.

OVERCOMING COMMON OBSTACLES

There are things that make it hard for parents to attend school events. The following is a list of those problems and some suggestions for dealing with them.

- *Parents who work and can't attend some events.* This is the most frequent reason why parents can't attend most school events, especially because both parents must now work in order to support the family. You may try reasoning with your employer, offering to make up the time lost on your own, or have it taken out of vacation or sick days. However, sometimes the situation can't be avoided. If that's the case, then let the school know that you want to attend the event, but can't. This tells the school that you are interested in what goes on. Many parents don't respond at all if they can't attend.This leads the school to believe they may not care or didn't receive the notice.

- *You've got small children at home and can't find a sitter.* This should not be a deterrent. In most cases, it is possible to bring the younger child to the school event with you. Don't forget, schools exist for the purpose of children. Some may offer day care while you're there. Also, this gives you a chance to expose your young child to the life of school. Take them along if possible.

- *Your spouse can't or won't go, and you don't want to go alone.* Having one parent attend is far better than having none at all, for your child's sake. Don't feel intimidated, you won't be alone. There will be many other single spouses or parents at the event. If you're a single parent, you'll be surprised at how many single parents there are at the event. Also, by letting the school know that you are a single parent, they'll do what they can to help you.

- *Your child didn't tell you about the event.* The number of announcements that make it home with the child diminishes in direct proportion with each higher grade. As older children get more involved in extra-curricular activities, they're more likely to lose announcements or forget to tell you. Many schools print up a monthly calendar that is available in the office, listing all events, closures and special days. You should also make it a habit to remind your children *daily* to bring home papers and announcements. Give them a backpack so that they can put the papers inside as they get them.

In every instance, you need to inform the school about obstacles that may be keeping you from attending conferences, meetings, and other events. Other parents will be having the same problem. As more and more families require two wage earners, the schools will have to accommodate the added pressures on parents in the way they schedule events.

HOW TO GET INVOLVED

There are many ways you can get involved with your child's teacher and school. Here's a list of some of them:

- *Join the PTA.* If you're new to this school business, PTA stands for "Parent-Teacher Association." This is a nationally supported organization, with local chapters at every school. It consists of a group of concerned parents who act as advocates for the children.

They generally meet once a month with several teachers that represent the faculty as well as the school's principal. Issues concerning discipline, equipment, extra-curricular activities, school curriculum and special programs are addressed. Some PTA's are more active than others. Some hold major fund raisers to provide special equipment, such as computers. Some publish school newsletters, hold recycling drives, bake sales and organize special field trips. Membership is generally very inexpensive, usually less than $10. This is an excellent way to get involved.

- *Be a Teacher's Aide.* Looking for part-time work? Then you may just be qualified to be a teacher's aide. Generally, you are given a very basic skills test and oral interview, then placed where teacher's aides are needed. You don't need teaching credentials or a college degree nor do you have to be there the whole day. Most positions are only for 3-4 hours. This is also a paid position.

- *Volunteer as a Room Mother or Father.* This position is most often available in kindergarten or the primary grades. If you have a day or two to spare, contact your child's teacher and offer your services as a Room Mother or Father. With as many as 30 five-year-olds to contend with, most kindergarten teachers jump at the chance, as do other teachers. A Room Mother or Father generally helps out with small groups of kids in arts and crafts, snack time, rest time, play time, trips to the school library, drink and bathroom requests, story time and generally allows the teacher to spend time working with smaller groups of children. This is an easy way to get involved.

- *Volunteer to help out with school events.* Bake sales, paper drives, Halloween night, jog-a-thon's, carnivals, fund raisers, field trips, drama clubs, music events—all are common events held by schools that depend on parent volunteers for support. Generally, you can volunteer for these events by contacting the school office or the PTA. Even if the events are sponsored by the PTA, you don't necessarily have to be a member to help out.

These are just a few of the many ways you can be involved in your child's school. Not only will you be expressing to your child that you are greatly concerned about his education, it also gives you the opportunity to have some say in how your child is educated. You may find yourself to be an instrument for changing the school, just because you demonstrated a need that others also had. Parents who speak up, voicing their positive, supportive attitudes about school, have a special impact. They will be seen as children whose parents are interested in their success in school.

Section III

Dealing with Practical Matters

7

Selecting the Best School and Teacher for Your Child

For the most part, you don't have much of a choice when it comes to selecting a public school for your child, and it is even more difficult to select a teacher. Public school educators generally don't like the public to have much choice in selecting schools and teachers. It tends to make efficient planning more difficult. There isn't any evidence that suggests parents make better choices than school people about the teachers and schools to whom their children are assigned. Nor is there much evidence that one teacher affects a child's ability to learn better than another.

However, some teachers are certainly better at it than others, although teachers' unions don't like to admit that fact; it implies that some teachers aren't very good. Teachers who are acknowledged to be less than adequate can stay in the classroom for many years and children must be assigned to them. Fortunately, only a small minority of teachers are seriously incompetent, but the problems they cause seem to make things difficult for many others. Sometimes you and your child may get caught in the crossfire and you're stuck with the worst teacher in the school for a whole year.

Teachers work under contracts that are negotiated by their union associations. These contracts deal with conditions of employment as well as wages. The contracts grant teachers certain rights which they formerly did not have. By increasing teachers' rights, there is a consequent reduction in the right of school administrators to arbitrarily decide many issues. Class size, teaching assignments, student assignments and many other issues that have to do with where a child is placed may be determined by contract. Parents don't have much say in the matter, except through their elected School Boards, who resolve these matters with teachers. School people are held accountable by law for upholding the contracts. You may lose some choices as a result.

Many schools are overcrowded. Overcrowding means that classes are larger than they should be and that schools cannot afford to hire the number of teachers or build enough classrooms to lower the student/teacher ratio on a more favorable scale. Students are apportioned according to where they live and the space and faculty available, so trying to attend a school not in your district is discouraged by the school administrators. This could mean your child will be placed in a school that may not offer the type of education he is best suited for.

Therefore, it isn't entirely unreasonable to suppose that some teachers and schools may be better for your child than others. The big problem is deciding who they are! No one has come up with a faultless system to "rate" or rank teachers. However, some states have school assessment programs that rank schools according to the results of tests given to students in various grades that assess skill levels in reading, writing and mathematics. Sometimes socio-economic factors are also part of the ranking. The scores can indicate how well the teachers are teaching. Some people place a lot of emphasis on these tests, others do not.

DETERMINE YOUR SCHOOL'S TEACHING METHODS

Schools differ in their teaching philosophies. You should determine how your school approaches teaching before you decide which school or teacher may be best for your child. Explore these issues in the spring of the school year before assignments for the next year are made. It is more likely that your preferences will be considered before a final decision has been made on assignments. After they have been made, the administrative issues regarding class size and distribution of students become difficult to change. Here is a list of things you can do to draw your own conclusions about the school in your area:

- Where does the school place the most emphasis on its curriculum?

- Contact the school your child is supposed to attend. Will the classes be taught in teams? Will there be more than one teacher who will be important to your child?

- Is your child going to be in a single grade or multi-grade classroom (more than one grade in the same room)? Who teaches it and how it's taught may be very important.

- What kind of support services and special programs does the school have? It is often these services that influence the schooling process more than individual teachers.

- What in-service support do teachers receive in the school? Good training programs help marginal teachers overcome their weaknesses.

- Finally, talk to parents whose children have attended the school you are supposed to attend. Ask them if they feel their children have been adequately taught. Ask them to relay experiences they've had with the school's principal, counselors and faculty. Parents, whose interests parallel your own, are often the best indicators.

CHOOSING ONE SCHOOL OVER ANOTHER

As mentioned before, requesting a school over another, especially if it's outside the district where you live, is discouraged by school administrators. After all, if everyone were allowed to choose freely, then some schools would be far more overcrowded than others. That's not to say it's impossible, but you generally must have a very good reason to request one school over another. Some of those reasons are:

- You work in another district and want your child to go to that school because it would be easier for you to transport him to and from school, as well as respond to any emergencies that may develop.

- There is more affordable (or available) child care near the other school as opposed to the one in your area.

- The other school offers special "Gifted and Talented" educational programs that your school doesn't and your child has been tested to show such ability.

- Your child has been tested with one or more learning disabilities and the other school is better equipped to deal with them.

- If you have a relative who lives in the other district, you could use that as the address to qualify for attendance at that school.

As I mentioned previously, you should contact the school district well in advance of the following school year before they set class assignments. Your chances for success will be greater.

CHOOSING THE "RIGHT" TEACHER

Once you've gotten the school assignment, you may have a preference for one teacher over another. How did you get information that one teacher was better than another? Gossip and reputation can't always be counted on. "Everyone says that Mrs. Jones is the best third grade teacher," may not be the most accurate assessment of what her capabilities really are. It would be fair to check with parents of other students who have had the teacher you're going to get to see how they felt about her.

Attending Classes

A better method is to see for yourself and sit in on several classrooms in the school year preceding your child's placement. Most schools will accommodate such requests. If the school is reluctant to permit it, a bit of pressure on the administrator, "I'm sure that your teachers have nothing to hide!" is likely to get you what you want. If you do sit in, here are some things to watch for:

- How well does the teacher hold the students' attention?

- How does the teacher handle discipline?

- Does the teacher communicate information on a level appropriate for the age/grade level of the children?

- How well does the teacher respond to questions by students?

- Is the teacher patient, courteous and respectful toward the students? Is she enthusiastic and appear to care greatly whether or not she is getting through to them?

- How much does the teacher encourage student participation?

- Do the students feel comfortable with the teacher or are they intimidated and hesitant to ask questions?

While you're observing, try to remain as objective as possible. Whether or not you *like* the teacher is important, although it doesn't mean she isn't well qualified and a good teacher for your child. If you don't like the teacher, it may build resentment and prevent you from having a good relationship with her, which will lead to problems throughout the school year. On the other hand, although she may exhibit some qualities you don't like, she may possess others that outweigh them. Nobody is perfect. Weigh the facts before you draw any conclusions.

If Your Child Has A Preference

Sometimes children may have preferences, especially if they have been at the school long enough to know the teachers. If your child has a strong preference for a teacher, you should explore the reasons why.

Matching your child's interests with the teacher's is tricky. You may believe that your child's interest in science is best served by a teacher who has a strong science program. But she may be planning to change her program during the year your child is in her room. Teachers change, experiment and adapt to the school's overall needs year by year.

Your child may be assigned to a new, first year teacher. You may wish to have an experienced teacher, a known quantity. Don't be hasty. Many young teachers bring enthusiasm, youth, flexibility and innovative ideas to a new job, making up for their lack of experience.

If you are concerned about your child's placement, see the school's administrator. Find out how the school decides where children will be assigned. Every school has some method for how they do it. Some schools have good assessment methods. You may be convinced that the school knows what it's doing. Lucky you! On the other hand you may feel that factors that are unique to your child are being overlooked. Talking to the administrator avoids putting your child's current teacher in the middle and enables you to impress the administrator with your concern. It's a good idea to have the administrator on your side.

Who your child has as a teacher is less important than the relationship your child has with that teacher. Sometimes a positive chemistry develops between a teacher and child that has nothing to do with the teacher's competence. Children who like their teacher and are liked in return will prosper even if the teacher is not the best in the school.

After school starts you will be able to make a better assessment of the teacher's actual relationship with your child. You may find your fears were unwarranted and your child is having a good year. If the match between your child and teacher is not working to your child's advantage, you can express your interest in having a change made. School people don't like to be found wrong, but they would rather not have irate parents badgering them. If, despite your sincere willingness to discuss the issue with the school and understand its position, you remain convinced that your child should be reassigned, continue to press your case. Your child's education is too important and you don't need to give up.

8

Helping Children with Homework

Developing good study skills right from the beginning is very important, as far as I'm concerned. I think children should have homework, although there are others who oppose this view. Despite the benefits, there are problems associated with homework, and many of them arise because parents don't know how to handle it. For homework to be an important element in the educational process, students, schools and parents each have an important role to play.

WHY HOMEWORK IS IMPORTANT

- Most of the material presented in school requires repetition, reinforcement and practice in order to be learned well. Homework is used to achieve this.

- Homework conveys the message that what is being done in school is important enough to do outside of school. If kids separate school from the rest of life, its importance soon diminishes.

- Homework shows you what your children are learning in school, and gives you an opportunity to monitor their progress.

- Homework in some subjects allows children to find applications for concepts that may not be possible to do at school. Sometimes assignments require children to take what they have learned in school and apply it to the "real world." In other words, homework is often used to expand the learning process.

- Homework involves you in your child's schooling by supporting, encouraging and emphasizing school's importance.

- Teachers use homework to gauge how well children are learning and use this information to adapt their teaching methods to best meet the needs of the child. That's why it's important for your child to do the homework without giving him too much assistance.

- Doing homework can become an important focus for family traditions and ceremonies. "Homework time" can be a way to organize schedules in the family.

- If you approach homework with the proper attitude and technique, your children will learn responsibility, persistence, organization, patience, work ethics and strategies for success.

WHAT YOUR ROLE SHOULD BE

As you prepare to help your child with homework, keep in mind that the *process* is more important than the *content*. The teacher and the student should bear the main responsibility for the content aspect of the homework. Your job is to facilitate the process by setting times, areas and by making yourself available to give advice and encouragement to your children. You don't necessarily need to understand what your children are trying to learn in order to help them learn to figure it out for themselves. The big trap to avoid: DON'T DO CHILDREN'S HOMEWORK FOR THEM. Most parents who try to help with homework allow kids to manipulate them into doing more than they should.

Developing Your Children's Study Skills

If you help your children with their homework correctly, they'll develop good study skills that they will use for the rest of their academic careers. How to go about helping them depends on the type of homework, the grade they are in and your children's special educational strengths and weaknesses. The following suggestions apply in most circumstances.

- Know the teacher's and school's policies and attitudes about homework. If the school expects homework to be done, then you can look for it most nights. If the teacher only gives homework for remediation, then you need to know when your child may have it. The more you know about the school's homework policies the better you will be able to help your child. Ask the teacher and the school administrator. If you doubt your child's insistence that he has no homework, or did it in school, call the teacher!

- Provide basic resources for homework to be done effectively. Space, time and material resources are your responsibility. Your children may do fine at the kitchen table, as long as the table is dedicated to homework for a reasonable period of time. Have a standard homework time, unless no homework has been assigned. Have paper, pencils and other school supplies available so that the lack of them cannot be used as an excuse to avoid an assignment.

- Children handle homework in a variety of ways. Some need absolute quiet, some like music. Some are easily distracted, some can do homework in the subway. Some even do homework while watching T.V. (I've seen it!), although I would discourage this method. It's important to understand each child's needs and provide that environment. Set aside space where your child may work uninterrupted.

- You should encourage children to do homework by themselves, rather than providing answers for them. This allows teachers to tell what children still don't know well enough. When your children ask for help, you should ask them more questions about the work rather than give answers. Have your children explain what they're supposed to be doing. Most textbooks have a logical format, which most children don't understand. Help them learn how to use the book, and allow your children to make mistakes! That is how they learn!

- Children must learn to trust themselves to be successful in school. When they learn to search out answers on their own, they will be more confident.

- Help your children keep calm when they're frustrated with the homework, the process, or with you (because you're not giving them answers). Counsel patience, "take a break," "take a deep breath and try again." Ask your children if they have solved a similar problem that can give them a clue. Suggest ways for them to stick with the task without creating power struggles.

- If your children have trouble with homework over a prolonged period of time, make an appointment with the teacher. You need to know what the results are in school; she needs to know what's happening at home. Stay in touch about homework problems.

- Avoid power struggles about the right answer or the right way to do something. Power struggles divert attention from the work to the relationship, which doesn't get the homework done! Many parents can't stand to see kids get the wrong answer. Don't be one of them.

- Use the homework study period as an opportunity to spend "quality time" with your children, although you have to be careful that this isn't the only period you spend quality time with them. If children don't want help, parents can feel rejected. Children may let the parent help even when they don't need it. Don't make homework a way to resolve family relationship issues.

- Let the school know that you support homework, and have no complaints about it being assigned frequently. Some teachers are reluctant to assign it because they believe that parents won't support them. Some teachers don't want the extra work that grading homework requires. When schools know what parents want, they often provide it, because they want parents' support. Some schools offer workshops to teach parents how to help children do homework. If yours doesn't, you might sponsor one at your school.

- If you want to reward your children for homework, reward them for their diligence, perseverance and their responsible behavior for completing it, not for doing the work correctly. Let the teacher and school do that. You should acknowledge efforts to control frustration, persist in the face of difficulties, stick with a hard task and meet the established deadlines.

- Children do homework successfully when they have met the teachers' standards and expectations, not yours. This is why it's important that you don't insist that children do homework the way you want them to. You have to understand what the teacher expects and become her agent in helping your children get their assignments done successfully.

9

Grades and Report Cards

If you want to see a good fight, put ten educators in a room and ask them to discuss the accuracy and importance of grades and report cards. One would think that there is general agreement about them since grading reports are universal in our educational system. There isn't! There is an intense debate going on in educational circles about grading. Some schools are doing away with traditional grading systems and experimenting with new ways to evaluate how well kids are doing. Unless that happens in your school district, you'll have to interpret the grades and report cards your child brings home as an indicator of how well they are doing.

HOW TEACHERS GRADE STUDENTS

You have to understand grades in order to interpret them and decide what they tell you about your child's progress. You can't understand what a grade means unless you understand the context from which it comes. Some teachers grade "hard," others "easy." Some grades reflect a child's performance relative to other children in the class, while some measure children against a predetermined standard. Some grades take into account your child's behavior. Others measure only what he has learned. Some teachers give higher grades as incentives, others give lower grades as warnings and/or incentives to do better. Some teachers give higher grades to children they like. Some kids "get the benefit of the doubt," others don't. Some teachers take grading seriously, others feel it's a joke. Some teachers have high standards, others have lower standards that qualify for the same grade. Sometimes the competition is keen and kids who normally get high grades get lower ones because it will look "funny" if everyone gets A's (just as it would look bad if everyone failed). But, despite knowing this, everyone wants children to get good grades.

THE IMPORTANCE OF GRADES

The educational issues about grades are confusing enough, but how children feel about them makes the situation even more complex. If children come home with "good" grades should they be rewarded? If so, then how? If children come home with "bad" grades, should they be punished, and if so, how? Sometimes parents and children don't judge the meaning or importance of grades similarly, which leads to conflict about them. Are grades a good way to measure whether children are succeeding in school? They are if parents or children think they are! Kids will be a lot happier in

45

school if they feel they're getting good grades and if their parents do too. Therefore, it's important to help your kids get good grades, if they want to. But, overall, you're on safer ground if you don't make too much of it, one way or another.

One of my children came to me once while in elementary school to seek an opinion. She wanted to know whether I thought that she could get all A's on her next report card. She tended to hover in that stratum, but had never quite achieved the straight-A level. She was shocked when I told her that I thought that she could, but didn't think that she should! I pointed out that there was no higher plateau to achieve, but falling off that plateau could lead to disappointment and frustration. As my children were prone to do, she thought my advice strange and proceeded to delight herself with straight A's during the last marking period.

Her teacher in the following year had a practice of not giving A's in the first marking period. My daughter got all B's and was crushed! It shook her confidence in her ability to control her own school performance. I didn't even have to say, "I told you so!"; she came to me and said it for me.

If children depend on good grades for feeling good about themselves, they're taking a big risk. If you depend on grades to tell you what your children are really learning, you may be disappointed.

HOW TO HANDLE GRADES AND REPORT CARDS

Despite all of this confusion, there are a number of things that you can do to ensure both you and your child will develop the right attitudes about grades.

- Find out how your child's teacher grades. Ask her about the grading system and procedures. Find out what children will have to do to get higher grades. Identify what factors she considers in determining grades. Discuss her point-of-view about the meaning and importance of grades. If she can't or won't give answers to these questions, you should be very careful about emphasizing them. You should also seek the opinion of her superior in order to identify the school's position on grades.

- Determine whether your child understands what will be required in order to get a good grade. If your child doesn't, then you and your child should meet with the teacher to make sure you all understand what's required.

- When your children bring their grades home find out if they know why they received those grades. If they don't, you should request a conference with the teacher, whether the grades were high or low.

- The grades that your child receives should not be a surprise. Stay

46

current with your child's performance, as much as possible, by reviewing work they bring home and staying in touch with the teacher.

- Ask your children how they feel about their grades before you tell them how *you* feel. Ask them if they would like to get different grades from what they achieved. Find out if they feel the grades are fair and accurate. Their answers can influence how you approach them and the teacher about grades. Sometimes children with low grades feel good about what they achieved while children with high grades don't. The goal is to help children evaluate their own performance and determine for themselves if the grades they got were what they deserved.

- The pattern of your children's grades is more important than any specific grade. If they have characteristically received high grades and suddenly they go down, find out why. If your child has characteristically not done well with grades and suddenly does, you need to discover the reason for it. In both instances you need to know whether the grade is truly indicative of performance or whether other factors are being considered.

- The grades that your children receive are less important than their overall feeling about school. This factor should never be overlooked, especially if they still feel good about school despite the fact they've received "bad" grades.

- Punishing a child for receiving poor grades is always inappropriate and usually ineffective. The key issues are whether children know what's required to raise the grades and whether you can create the circumstances that will help them do so. Sometimes the process may feel like punishment, e.g. less T.V. and more time devoted to homework.

- Families have different traditions about whether to reward children for good grades. Paying children for grades is controversial and may not prove useful in the long run. As children move higher in schooling, they may choose higher grades ("cinch" courses) over challenging opportunities (honors programs where the competition is keener). If you choose to reward children for good grades, pick a method that involves overall achievement rather than individual grades. It places the emphasis where it should be.

- It's important to make a distinction between actual performance and grades. Your children may get average grades but are making steady progress relative to their past performance. Grades don't often measure how far a child has come. You should have other ways to measure your children's progress, including direct observation and conferencing with the teachers.

Getting good grades is one way to determine if your children are being successful in school, but other measures are better. It's more important for your child to enjoy school and be interested in what he is doing. Nevertheless, as long as the system does grading, it's a good idea to know how to get good ones. Know what the teacher wants and provide her with it. Hard-working students who understand what the teacher requires will often get better grades than children of high intellect who don't care.

Help your children learn how to get good grades. As children learn strategies for improving their grades, they will learn to separate their emotions from their grades, allowing curiosity, interests, their own standards and personal goals to have more influence on their performance.

Section IV

Handling Problems that Interfere with Success in School

10

When Kids Complain about School

It is somewhat natural for your child to complain about school. It goes with the territory. But you need to be careful about how you interpret your child's complaints, to make sure there isn't a more serious, underlying reason that indicates something isn't going well at school; something you will need to do something about.

Children usually complain about school for several reasons: because something or someone is truly bothering them; because they want to cover up for something more serious; or because they want your attention. Exactly what it is that is bothering a child may not have anything to do with school, even though the complaint is directed at it. Some of the complaints may reflect normal childhood struggles that are all part of a child's healthy development. Regardless of the reason, you need to pay attention to their complaints so they don't get the idea you don't care. You must learn to identify whether or not the complaints stem from a real problem at school.

Most children can't accurately describe things that bother them. School-as-a-whole ("I just don't like it!") is an easy target, as is "school is unfair," especially because parents are not on the scene. If you want sympathy, complain about something that people can't check out. Parents want children to be happy, but complaining about school where parents have little control is a good way to elicit concern. Kids do things like that!

WHEN YOUR CHILD COMPLAINS ABOUT FAIRNESS

It is rare that a child goes through school without feeling that he or she is being treated unfairly. There are a variety of reasons why they may feel that way. Schools are large bureaucracies and try as they might, they can't always treat everyone the same way. You may have one child who is one of thousands that must be managed by a complex system of rules, procedures, policies and regulations. Therefore, there are times when unfair treatment will occur.

One of the situations where unfair treatment occurs is called the *Rule of Second*. This is where a child does something "second," often reacting to something done to him first. One child does something to another while the teacher is not watching. The "done to" child makes an observable reaction, attracting the teacher's attention, who sees the child lash back in some way, without having seen the original perpetrator. The second child receives the punishment, despite vigorous protests, because the "perp" denies all knowledge of the event. Of course, this is understandably an unfair situation and it occurs frequently in school.

Teachers are human and they are going to be unfair sometimes. Despite illusions about teachers being super-human, they do have faults. One of them is a human tendency to treat children unequally. Some children are treated with favoritism while others are barely tolerated. When a teacher develops a negative impression about a child, that child becomes labeled and the teacher becomes sensitized to behavior that reinforces the label. If children develop bad reputations, it's hard for them to live it down. They will often get blamed for things they didn't do nor initiate.

Life is frequently unfair! Therefore, your children must develop effective methods to combat this fact. They need to learn that unfairness does not have to be tolerated. At the same time, they must learn not to "cry wolf" every time they are faced with unfair treatment.

OTHER REASONS WHY CHILDREN COMPLAIN

The reasons that children complain about school have validity, but only some of them are about school itself. Many complaints about school reflect normal childhood struggles which schools and teachers get blamed for. Here are some reasons why your child may complain about school:

- Your child is having difficulty getting along with the teacher, the subject matter, school rules or is being treated unfairly.

- Other children may be picking on your child. Perhaps your child is teased frequently, bullied, excluded from group play or victimized in some manner by other children. Self interest and loyalty to friends are motives that create groups of "insiders and outsiders." Winning at all costs, emotional disabilities and simple selfishness incline kids to treat each other unfairly. Perhaps the teachers may not be aware of what's happening or your child is afraid to tell them to protect himself or his friends.

- If your child is in grades K-2, then he may be suffering from separation anxiety. He may be frustrated about having to share attention with 29 other children, or perhaps your child doesn't have adequate social skills to get along in the classroom. In these cases, your child may complain in general, about feeling sick at school.

- Some children handle frustration better than others. Your child may be having difficulty learning new material and can't identify the problem. Therefore, your child may complain about something else, such as "The teacher is always picking on me."

- Older children who have lost leadership roles, have had friends move away, don't have a consistent friendship group, or are finding that other children do better than they at school begin to complain about almost anything. School is terribly uncomfortable for them because they have no valued role. The school or teacher is blamed because the child feels cut off and uncomfortable when at school.

- Your children may complain about school just to get your attention and sympathy. They may feel a loss because a sibling was born, a parent started a new job or other events have disturbed family life and reduced the attention you normally give that child. Complaining about school is a way to see if you really care about them.

- Children may have a fear of failing even if they are successful. Vague, generalized, pervasive feelings of fear and anxiety affect most children from time to time. They are even more anxious because they can't tell why they're feeling so bad. School is stressful so it receives the blame.

- Teachers are not mind readers. Even though children complain about apparently significant events, the teacher may not be aware of their feelings. Kids hide their feelings. They may be fearful of the reaction to their complaint. In many instances, the teacher may be able to "fix" the situation if she knows about it.

WHAT YOU CAN DO

Here are a number of things you can do when your child complains about school:

- *Talk and listen.* Accept what your child says without judgment and encourage him to speak freely in order to get a complete picture of what the complaint is about. There will always be gaps in his story. Uncover the history of the situation, and determine who the players are.

- *Provide guidance.* Try to steer your child into taking responsibility for solving the problem on his own. Ask, "What do you think can be done about it?" "How do you think the problem should be solved?" "Have you discussed this with any of your friends at school?" Often, this procedure will dissolve the complaint and lead you and your child to the root of the problem.

- *What do you want me to do?* is a logical next question if the

53

discussion needs to continue. Sometimes children want to complain, but don't really want parents to get involved. Their wishes should be tested.

- *Check with the school.* When to call or visit the school depends on the seriousness of the complaint and whether or not the child has asked you to intervene. If you feel the complaint is serious enough, you should contact the school over the child's objections. You should schedule a meeting between you, your child and the teacher. You should not exempt your child from confronting an unfair teacher. Having your child confront his teacher about unfairness will help him learn to cope with stressful situations.

- *Explore the issues.* The meeting between you, your child and the teacher should be focused on exploring the issues, not fixing blame. Even if the complaint has no objective basis, you should not blame your child for "crying wolf." There may be other emotional reasons that the complaint was made. They need to be explored.

- *Make a plan.* Help your child identify what to do the next time. You may discover that the complaint has no objective basis, no one did anything. But the child still felt the need to complain, so what should he do the next time he feels bad? How should he handle it, so that he doesn't feel cut off from caring adults nor embarrassed to show his feelings?

- *Check in.* Ask your child, from time to time, how things are going, especially about the issues that came to the surface through the above process. Show interest, but don't be a nag! Don't complain about his complaining! Coming to terms with the pressures of life is no less difficult for children than adults.

If you have a comfortable relationship with your children's teachers, dealing with complaints is much easier. The teachers know you and are more willing to respond to your concerns. They will also be more honest and candid with you.

WHAT TO DO IF YOUR CHILDREN DON'T COMPLAIN

As a final note, there are some signs that you should pay attention to that may indicate your children are having a difficult time in school, but they are *not* complaining about it. These are signs that you should contact the teacher to compare experiences you're having.

- Your child either doesn't talk about school or he gives evasive answers about it, even to the most specific questions. Slight pressure from you to talk about school results in emotional outbursts.

- Your child suddenly avoids something that he used to love to do.

- Your child *never* complains about school, always bathing it in a positive glow. This may be evidence that they are avoiding dealing with issues. Sometimes children are afraid to talk about negative things that they are struggling with for fear that they will open a Pandora's box which they can't handle.

- Your child begins to ask questions about drugs, sex, or other significant problems without specifying the source of his interest. Things may be going on at school that he is reluctant to talk about or he doesn't wish to break a confidence.

- Your child suddenly avoids going to school, starts complaining about being ill, spends a lot of time in the nurse's office and seems to be under stress from sources that are unclear to you.

If you're involved with the school, staying in touch with your children's teachers and keeping lines of communication open, you will be in a better position to evaluate your children's complaints. You will be in a good position to help solve significant problems, removing serious obstacles that may prevent them from being successful in school.

11

When the School Complains about Your Child

The school may have complaints about your children. They may not have turned out to be the brilliant, angelic creatures you hoped for! Or they may be spunky, individualistic, and unwilling to knuckle under to "the system." Handling complaints about children is a big subject. The complaints and the school's attitudes and standards can be so varied and complex. A few guidelines will be useful in a variety of situations.

First of all, there is a difference between a school's *complaint* and a school's *concern*. Teachers may sincerely be concerned about a child's performance or behavior that requires asking the parents to become involved. This may not be a complaint so much as an effort to solve a problem that is interfering with that child's ability to succeed.

A complaint, however, is registered because a child's performance or behavior is interfering with other people's ability to function or the child has broken rules, standards or regulations. Complaints need to be taken seriously because how your child is perceived at school will influence his ability to be successful.

WHY SCHOOLS COMPLAIN ABOUT CHILDREN

The school's chief issue with "problem children" is that they disrupt the system that is required to maintain order in the school. Schools will complain when:
- Your child resists authority
- Victimizes other children
- Is consistently disrespectful toward adults
- Brings illegal items or substances onto school grounds
- Destroys school property
- Demonstrates poor impulse control
- Refuses to conform to school rules and participate in activities

Some schools handle infractions in these areas with the children, before parents are contacted. Others react quickly and call in parents, sometimes before all the evidence is in.

It is likely that what the school is complaining about, if not resolved, will interfere with the child's ability to be successful in that school. Even if the

57

school has a valid complaint about a child, the goal is to establish the conditions in which the child can be successful in school. If the school's complaint is not valid, in your opinion, then it's important to re-establish the child's credibility in order to insure future success.

What To Do

Here are suggestions that can help in either instance, whether or not you agree with the school:

- Get to the root of the matter by listening to both sides of the story—your child's and the school's. All the parties will need to meet at some point in order to confront the issues that are raised. It is best if you and your child attend such a meeting together.

- The goal is to align the perceptions of everyone involved in the situation. Unless everyone sees the situation similarly solutions will be tentative and unsatisfactory.

- Fixing blame usually proves fruitless, not because people lie, but because situations are usually more ambiguous than anyone supposes. Even if children have broken a school rule, it is likely that they did so for reasons that make sense, at least to them. But if the situation requires punishment according to school regulations, don't exempt guilty parties, including your child, from the consequences.

- The school should see you as a fair-minded advocate for your child. You need to sort out what your child is responsible for and admit it. Your child should not come away from the situation feeling victimized, but he should also be aware of his responsibility. Unless your child has been a chronic offender, the school will wish to avoid victimizing him.

- Solutions and agreements are needed. What will stop this situation from occurring in the future? What does everyone, including you, your child, the teachers and other children, have to do to resolve the problem? Everyone involved in the situation has some role to play to insure it doesn't happen again. As the parent, you need to clarify what the school expects of you.

- Clarify what you need to do at home to deal with the situation and what the school is going to do. Establish lines of communication and check-in times when you or the school will contact the other. Do not leave it unclear. It helps children control their behavior if they know that contact between home and school will occur.

- If you are satisfied that the punishment that the school is imposing is fair, than you don't need to add to it at home. If you wish to reinforce the school's sanctions with restrictions at home do so only for a limited period.

- If you feel that the school's handling of the situation is unfair, wrong or insensitive to the needs of your child or yourself, you don't need to knuckle under. It shows that you have not formed effective relations with the school personnel, teachers or administrators. The goal is not to "get" the school, it is to find a way to establish a relationship in which your voice can be heard and your child's needs can be addressed.

- You catch more flies with honey than vinegar! It's an awful cliche, but true nonetheless in this context. There are times when you have to go to bat for your children in the face of the school's opposition. Sometimes you can only get what your child needs by demands and threats. Fortunately, these are rare occurrences. Parents who get advantages for the children in quiet, friendly and cooperative ways do not make news. Parents who have to "go to the mat" with schools and teachers have usually not spent time building positive relationships with the people involved. Having the school know you is like having an insurance policy. You may not have to cash it in for a while, but the resources will be there when you need them.

School is where children seek to establish their own identity and independence from parental control. It is also a place in which the stresses of growing up are played out. Good schools and good teachers understand this. They may fully understand the developmental needs that resulted in your child's misbehavior, but they are required to maintain the integrity of the school as a system. It is at such points that the school may feel that an individual's needs must give way to school rules and regulations. The school needs to have the child fit into the system; your goal as a parent is to trim the system to fit your child. Handling school complaints is one more area in which this paradox is played out. No one need be a victim in the process.

12

When Children and Teachers Don't Get Along

I am in awe of most teachers, especially those who have taught for a number of years. They have found a way to get along with hundreds of children year after year, liking the kids in their classes and being liked by them. Some go beyond the ordinary and have loving relationships with their students. They are long remembered by former students and colleagues. How fortunate the child who has had such a teacher. So many teachers have such good relationships with children that we are surprised, disappointed, and even angered when a child and his teacher don't get along. We forget that teachers and children are only human. Sometimes they don't like each other, even though they're supposed to.

Therefore, the possibility exists that your child and his teacher will misunderstand each other and develop conflicts. Here are some reasons why that may occur:

- The relationship started off wrong and never got on track.

- There is a "personality conflict" in which the teacher and/or your child keep attacking characteristics in the other that can't be changed.

- The teacher has taken a punitive stance toward your child resulting in criticism or punishments that are unfair and unwarranted.

- The teacher may have said things to your child that were hurtful or demeaning and your child hasn't been able to forgive or forget.

- Your child has made some effort to adjust to the situation or even improve it but to no avail. The conflict remains and involves power struggles, bad communication and produces anxiety in your child.

Hopefully, these are situations that occur rarely. Such a relationship can have a profound impact on your child's feelings about school and may have lasting effects. You need to address the situation before permanent damage is done.

HOW TO HANDLE THE SITUATION

How to handle such situations will vary relative to the grade and school

61

level your child is in. Very small schools may have limited alternatives. It's a delicate situation in which you need to approach with caution. But, being cautious does not mean that you can't be persistent and decisive in protecting your child's interests.

I will assume that you and your child have discussed the situation and it has not improved. You should have contacted the teacher when your child first complained about the relationship, but you are not satisfied that repairs have been made. You feel that neither child nor teacher is able to adjust enough to improve the situation.

Your Child's Involvement

If your child is in grades K-3, you may not wish to involve him in your dealings with the issue. Your child may be anxious and fearful of repercussions from the teacher if he pursues it. You will have to be your child's spokesman and advocate. However, if your child is in the upper grades and older, you should involve him. He needs to be challenged to confront issues that affect his life directly, with your support, encouragement and presence. Children in the elementary grades should not be required to confront severe chronic problems between them and a teacher on their own. They will be at a considerable disadvantage.

You may have to make the hard decision about how much you trust your child's reports. If you and the child have a history of honesty and confidence in your relationship, you have a distinct advantage. If not, you need to be careful that you aren't hoping that "fighting for your child" will be a way to regain the child's confidence in you. I will presume that you believe the child. If you don't, the problem may be with you and your relationship with your child, not his relationship with his teacher.

Talk To The Teacher And Principal

The teacher needs to know what your child has told you and how you perceive the situation. Serious discussion with the teacher may produce a positive change. You need to decide whether you trust the teacher's reports about events at school. If you can't, request that you and the teacher meet with the school's principal. If you do not know the principal, call him or her ahead of time, introduce yourself, explain why you and the teacher are meeting with her and indicate that you wish to find a good solution to the problem. This is very important because if you are angry, tell the principal what you want her to do and reduce her options, you will be faced with hostile resistance. You might not get a fair hearing. How the principal handles your child in this process will tell you a lot about whether she will be an advocate for your child.

The meeting between you, the teacher and the principal is also important because it signifies that you and the teacher are unable to resolve the matter. The age and attitude of the child will determine whether he should be present in these meetings. At the conclusion of this meeting you will decide whether you trust the teacher enough to continue to seek solutions while your child remains in her class. If you don't, seek a transfer of the child to another teacher.

Transferring To Another Teacher

Initially, the school may take the position that the child cannot be moved, usually for administrative reasons (class size, teacher contracts, school policies). Many parents give up at this point, especially if dealing with a large system that seems impervious to their demands. Don't believe it; school administrators want to keep the peace, you still have power! Your response should be, "If not now, when?", "If not here, where?", "What is the process for appealing your decision about the regulations?". By taking this stance, you're telling the school that your child's education is important to you and you're not about to give up.

If you feel that you are being stonewalled, lied to, or not supported by the school's administration, you should consider going to the next administrative level in the school district, following the same procedure. Call ahead, introduce yourself, explain the situation as you see it, indicate your wish to find an acceptable solution. You can also write to the District Superintendent and send a copy of your complaint to someone on the school board. Many administrators get nervous when a school board member's name appears on a complaint letter they have received. Those letters usually get immediate attention!

If you have gone this far, it is likely that a solution will be found. Most school's do not want angry parents who will mobilize others to fight the school system. Your goal is to find someone in the system with whom you feel comfortable and whom you identify as a partner in having your child's well-being as the chief concern—not the teacher's or the system's.

13

When Your Child Seems Scared to Go to School

Many children have periods when they are scared to go to school. This shouldn't be too surprising, because school can be a stressful and intimidating place for a young child. It's a rare child who hasn't experienced some anxiety about school and tried to avoid going.

Some fears have to do with what they experience there, or on the way to school. But many fears about going to school have underlying reasons that may not be directly related to school. Being afraid to go to school falls under the psychological label of "school phobia." It's best to avoid that label because it implies that there is a specific "disease" for which there is a specific "cure." Your first step should be to understand what is happening with your child.

WHY CHILDREN GET SCARED

- Your child may not be able to cope with the stresses of a teaching/learning situation or interacting with other children socially. He may be intimidated by the size of the school and overwhelmed by the vast number of children.

- Your child may have a distorted view about what's going on. He may have blown out of proportion the teacher's attitude, or developed unfounded fears about bigger or older kids. He may see threats in situations no one else does.

- Your child may be anxious about his school performance and has a heightened fear of failure. He may have trouble keeping up with the work and fears the consequences.

- The child is being bullied by other children, with or without the teacher's knowledge and doesn't know how to get them to stop. He could be fearful to tell you because they have threatened him with harm.

- Other children or adults are stopping your child on the way to or from school and mistreating him, creating fear and anxiety.

- Your child may not be able to cope with the fact he is no longer the center of attention as he was at home before starting school.

65

He can not deal with his frustration at not getting what he wants or having things go his way.

- Your child may be experiencing separation anxiety. He has not been away from home and parents before and has few skills to cope with the situation.

- If your family is going through a crisis, such as a severe illness or injury, divorce or some other problem, your child may be afraid to leave home for fear that something awful will occur while he is gone.

- A child may fear that something bad will happen to his parent (usually the mother) while he's gone. He perceives her as depending on him for emotional support or assistance. He feels overly responsible for things at home.

These are some of the reasons why your child may be frightened to go to school. This situation is complicated when children can not distinguish between things that are real and objective, and those that are distortions or clouded by emotional issues. Many children cannot clearly identify what it is that makes them afraid to go to school, either not knowing or fearing to admit it.

Children may indirectly communicate fears about school. They may complain about vague illnesses or feelings. They may have a hard time sleeping or waking. They may develop problems around food.

Children can't be successful at school if they don't get there enough. But, it is important that they be comfortable when they are at school. If they are suppressing fears and dragging themselves off to school to avoid punishment, their ability to learn will be limited. While it's important to have them overcome fears and attend school, it's also important to understand the causes of their anxieties.

WHAT YOU SHOULD DO

Although I can not diagnose what your child may be experiencing with regard to fears about school, I do have a number of suggestions for you to consider.

- When your child expresses fears, listen carefully and remain as calm as possible. Do not dismiss his fears as minor or imagined. The fact is, these fears can be very real in your child's mind. Take your child's fears seriously.

- Your goal is to determine what your child feels is needed to help him get to school. A calm, dispassionate discussion may solve the problem if it has not gone too far.

- If your child wants you to take him to school, and it is possible for you to do so, determine the limited number of times you will do so and keep reminding your child of that limit. If it is not possible (because of work schedules, etc..) clearly indicate that it isn't and seek an alternative. Perhaps you can arrange for other mothers of his classmates to take your child to school.

- You should try to get your child to overcome his fears himself. This means that you are persistently seeking an answer to the question, "What is it that you need from me (or from the teacher or from others) that will make you feel more comfortable about going to school?"

- Limit your assistance as much as possible with certain conditions. For instance, start by walking your child to school for a few days, then change it to just walking him to the bus or halfway for a few days more, withdrawing your assistance gradually until you finally stop. Give your child a sense of security by being with him, but don't make him overly dependent on it. It is important to form a "coalition" with your child to help him get past his fears, especially when they arise from emotional sources.

- If your child insists that the fear results from real events occurring at school you should contact the teacher. The teacher may be able to help him cope with situations at school.

- If avoiding school has to do with stresses or crises at home, develop methods by which anxiety can be reduced. Talk over the home situation with your child in ways that are appropriate for his age and development. Find out what he is fearing. A good idea is to call him at school during the day to reassure him that you or other family members are okay.

- Do not let your child stay home from school just because he is scared. This avoids, rather than confronts, the problem. If your child's fears are highly irrational and he is extremely emotional, you should seek professional help by asking the school to make a recommendation. Most school districts have their own psychologists.

Fear is a part of growing up. All children develop fear about something. School can activate many of the normal fears inherent in children. Social pressures, success and failure, separation from nurturing, new duties and responsibilities and the absence of loved ones can make school a difficult place to be. However, many school fears can disappear quickly if your child is made to feel like he is understood and accepted. He needs to be reassured that you're there giving support and that he has the power to overcome his fears if he tries hard enough. Give him the reassurance.

14

How to Deal with Divorce

It's unfortunate that divorce is now almost as commonplace as marriage. Despite this fact, many schools act as if children still have two parents living at home, when many of them don't. Divorced parents, especially non-custodial ones, are responsible for staying involved in their children's education. When they do so in the right way, children can be helped to be successful in school.

Divorces range from those in which the former spouses remain in friendly communication to those in which anger, resentment and mistrust are so deep that joint efforts to support children's education are impossible. When custody is in dispute, schools often become battlegrounds for the parents. It is widely believed that the people who suffer most in any divorce are the children, and nowhere can the effects of divorce be seen better than at school.

The paradox is that the more a divorced couple can act as if they are happily married, the better it will be for the child. This means that they must communicate openly, have similar values and attitudes about schooling, attend school events, meet with teachers together and provide consistent support to the child. Most married couples don't do those things very well! You are fortunate if your divorce has resulted in that kind of mutual commitment to your child's schooling.

WHAT TO AVOID

There are some things that you should avoid doing if both you and your ex-spouse wish to stay involved in your child's schooling.

- Don't require your children to have to deal with the divorce at school, such as having to ask for two of everything that goes home, sorting out which papers will go to Dad and which to Mom and attending double teacher conferences.

- Don't require your children to call the parent with whom they're not living every day to report on how school went (not even every other day).

- Be aware that young children will agree to almost any request their divorced parents make in the hope that doing so might make peace or ultimately bring them back together. Such fantasy wishes last a long time, making it appear that children are comfortable

71

doing things that they really hate to do.

- The school performance of most children suffers during the divorce and for some time afterward. Becoming punitive, critical, demanding or putting pressure on for improvement can add terrible burdens to an already stress-filled situation. Trying to meet the different standards set by you and your ex is more than most kids can handle.

- If you and your spouse are not communicating, don't ask your children to be the bridge, even if it's only about school matters. Just because they are willing to talk with both of you does not mean that they should be spokesman for either one of you.

- Don't put the school or teacher in the middle. Parents who are not communicating often "make deals" with the school to inform them about their children. Schools don't know who has custody or what the formal agreements are, unless you let them know. The school does not want the child victimized by the parents. The school does not know which parent should have what information. If the school has to go to the children to sort things out, the children become responsible for something they shouldn't be.

The reason for not doing the things just mentioned is that it makes school uncomfortable and stressful for children, reducing their motivation to be successful. When negative feelings become attached to school from these pressures, children cannot feel much satisfaction. They begin to feel as if school is the source of their pain and discomfort, since they don't wish to blame their parents. Loyalty to parents and fantasies about family reunification result in the school being blamed. Young children of divorced parents tend to deny their parent's faults.

Despite these problems, both parents can stay involved in educational matters after the divorce, even if they don't like each other. Hopefully, you both care enough about your children to put aside your differences and exercise self-control to avoid putting your child in a compromising position.

WHAT YOU SHOULD DO

- Inform the school of both parent's addresses and request that mailed notices be sent to both. If you are a non-custodial parent and don't live in the area, a good idea is to provide the school with self-addressed, postage-paid envelopes so they can send copies of notices and reports to you.

- Let the teacher and principal know that both parents are available in emergencies and provide both work and home numbers.

- If possible, let the school know what the custody conditions are so that it can fulfill it's legal obligations as well as meeting the children's needs.

- Try to keep your children in the same school they were attending prior to the separation. People know them and can care for their emotional needs. Also, because their home life is now unstable, school becomes the only constant in their lives. Your children need that stability and security now more than ever.

- Insure that at least one parent attends all school functions. If you can't stand to be in the same room, decide who will attend. Give the other parent the opportunity to attend if, at the last minute, you are unable to. Knowing that a parent will attend every event gives children a feeling of consistency and security.

- Have resources for completing homework and doing school projects at both parents homes, if you both live in the same area. Knowing that they will not be exempted from doing homework when visiting parents provides a feeling of continuity about school and reinforcement about its importance.

- Set up a "School Fund" to which both parents contribute from which special expenses (school trips, etc.) are taken. It helps children value school to know that both parents value it enough to pay for it. Even if school expenses are to be covered by child support payments, the "School Fund" makes children feel that both parents are pitching in.

- If divorced parents, who agree on nothing else, can work together with regard to their children's schooling, the school takes on added significance for children. This is because they view it as an arena in which the parents are "together." Doing well in school allows children to satisfy both parents simultaneously, an opportunity that the children may have in no other way. Deep, unconscious wishes for bonding as a family can be, in part, satisfied by parental agreements about school. If both parents can stay involved in the right way, children feel that school is a source of comfort, not pain. Their chances of succeeding are greatly enhanced.

15

THE LAST WORD

Schools can be strange places. Often times it is hard to make sense of what happens in them. Students are constantly asked to do things that they don't know how to do, and when they finally figure out how to do it, they're given something new to do that they haven't yet learned. They have to meet standards set by strangers, not Mom and Dad, and they can't influence them. Much of what children do in school seems to have no immediate purpose, quite different from the rest of their lives where most things are done for concrete reasons. If they ask why they have to do something, the answer is that it's preparation for the future, about which children aren't well informed. For many children school makes little sense. They need help from teachers and their parents, because if they start out badly, it's harder to correct as they get older.

This book has been about how parents can help their children understand school and succeed in what school asks of them. One reason that parents don't involve themselves in their children's education is because the school makes no more sense to them than it does to children. But parents have the ability to overcome that problem and help their children in the process.

Parents who don't have a sense of responsibility about their children's schooling will instill the same attitude in their children. It is difficult for children to take things seriously if their parents don't, especially when they are very young and forming attitudes about school and their place in it. In all of the current discussion about schooling in American society, the simple factor of parental interest as a critical ingredient in school performance sometimes gets lost.

The public blames the schools for children's poor performance. The schools blame the parents and the public-at-large for not supporting the schools with time and money. Both are right, but only in that professional educators cannot do the job without parents active support, no matter how much money they have to work with. Parental involvement in their children's education is the critical ingredient. Most studies of schools demonstrate it again and again. It's a simple idea, perhaps too simple.

Some children seem to catch fire about learning without the active support of their parents. It's a small proportion that do. Don't depend on your children's innate love of learning to make them successful in school. For most people, love of learning comes later in life, often after leaving school. In the early years it's more likely that children will be successful if they have a good sense of responsibility and a workman-like attitude toward

74

school. If they are motivated to do well in school, they will find a way, with your support.

This book did not address the special issues of children with learning or physical handicaps, or children who are gifted and talented in schools designed for more ordinary intellects. I did not discuss the issues that race or equity present, nor the special problems of sex discrimination that often are present in elementary schooling.

However, the issues that are discussed in this Handbook will help in handling these special problems in any situation you find yourself and your children. Handicapped children as well as gifted ones, poor children, foreign born, and minority children—all share one important characteristic—they are children! The stresses of schooling are similar for them. The solutions also have common characteristics. When a mentally handicapped child and a normal functioning one complain about school, the process for dealing with their complaints is similar, while the details may vary.

Many people who have read other works in the *Whole Child Series* may be wondering why I didn't discuss self-esteem, perhaps the most critical ingredient to ensure your child's success in school. The reason is simply that the subject is so important that it should be, and is, addressed in a book of its own, *How To Raise Children's Self-Esteem* of the *Whole Child Series*. However, many of the suggestions in this Handbook will help children improve and maintain their self-esteem. Even children with good self-esteem need to be reassured in order to remain successful in school.

Being involved in children's schooling can be fun! You meet interesting people, both parents and educators. You become a learner along with your children. Schools belong to parents, just as they do to children. Don't let your children keep you out. They have no idea how much they will lose if you aren't involved in their schooling.

Schools are also competitive arenas, where we train children to cope with the forces of our democratic and free market society. Because of this, some children will be winners and others will be losers. However, it is possible, to make sure there are considerably more winners than losers. Parents can tip the scales and provide support for their children that puts them in the winner's column.

At the time that this book is being written, the world is going through profound changes that will have a lasting effect on the fabric of our country. It is growing more difficult to predict what the world will be like, what demands will have to be faced, and what skills will be needed by the children who are presently starting school. One thing remains fairly consistent, though. Children who are successful in school have a much better chance of being successful later in life. Wouldn't you like to be able to improve the odds for your children?

THE WHOLE CHILD SERIES

WHOLE CHILD books offer practical techniques for dealing with children. Written in an easy-to-understand, straightforward style, this series of books offers sound advice from family counselors in areas most important to healthy childhood development.

HOW TO TEACH CHILDREN RESPONSIBILITY
Helps you to define responsibility and provides practical activities for developing a strong sense of responsibility in your child.

HOW TO DISCIPLINE CHILDREN WITHOUT FEELING GUILTY
Tips on how to direct children by rewarding good behavior, fitting chores to the child and how to be consistent and fair-minded with discipline.

HOW TO RAISE CHILDREN'S SELF-ESTEEM
Focuses on helping children to improve self-confidence, values, attitudes and their ability to interact with others.

HOW TO RAISE TEENAGERS' SELF-ESTEEM
Includes new approaches to dealing with problems faced by teens, analysis of self-esteem difficulties and advice on how to help teenagers raise their own self-esteem.

HOW TO HELP YOUR CHILD SUCCEED IN SCHOOL
A guide to dealing with the practical issues of schooling; how to develop an early desire to learn, dealing with teachers, selecting schools and handling problems that interfere with children's success in school.

HOW TO BE A SLIGHTLY BETTER PARENT
A simple, no-nonsense guide to improving your skills as a parent and your relationship with your children.

All books in the *Whole Child Series* may be purchased wherev
or direct from the publisher.

PRICE STERN SLOAN
11150 Olympic Boulevard
Suite 650
Los Angeles, California 90064